FORTUNE SELF-PUBLISHING

Expert Secrets & Strategies to Sell More Books, Make Money Online & Earn Passive Income for Authors, Entrepreneurs & Beginners

William Swain

© COPYRIGHT 2022 - ALL RIGHTS RESERVED.

The content contained within this book may not be reproduced, duplicated, or transmitted without direct written permission from the author or the publisher.

Under no circumstances will any blame or legal responsibility be held against the publisher, or author, for any damages, reparation, or monetary loss due to the information contained within this book, either directly or indirectly.

Legal Notice:
This book is copyright protected. It is only for personal use. You cannot amend, distribute, sell, use, quote, or paraphrase any part, or the content within this book, without the consent of the author or publisher.

Disclaimer Notice:
Please note the information contained within this document is for educational and entertainment purposes only. All effort has been executed to present accurate, up-to-date, reliable, and complete information. No warranties of any kind are declared or implied. Readers acknowledge that the author is not engaged in the rendering of legal, financial, medical, or professional advice. The content within this book has been derived from various sources. Please consult a licensed professional before attempting any techniques outlined in this book.

By reading this document, the reader agrees that under no circumstances is the author responsible for any losses, direct or indirect, that are incurred as a result of the use of the information contained within this document, including, but not limited to, errors, omissions, or inaccuracies.

https://www.subscribepage.com/fortunepublishing

Or scan the QR code below.

Contents

INTRODUCTION 1

THE MOST IMPORTANT STEP 5

- BRAINSTORM 5
- BOOKBEAM 6
- CATEGORY SEARCH 7
- METRICS 8
- SCORE 10

STEP 2: OUTLINING 13

- OUTLINE STEPS 14
- CREATING THE OUTLINE 16

STEP 3: PROFESSIONAL BOOK WRITING 21

- THE URBAN WRITERS 22
- THE WRITING SUMMIT 23
- HOT GHOST WRITER 24
- UPWORK 24
- FIVERR 25
- CHECKING YOUR PROJECT 25

STEP 4: TITLES THAT SELL 27

- LIST THE BENEFITS 28
- KEYWORDS 31
- SAMPLE YOUR STORY 32
- COMMON PHRASES 32
- EMOTIONAL TRIGGER WORDS 32

STEP 5: BEST SELLING DESCRIPTION 35

- FORMATS 35
- HEADLINE 36

STEP 6: CREATING A COVER 39

- FINDING DESIGNERS 39
- BACK COVER 41
- AUDIBLE COVER 41

STEP 7: BEAUTIFUL FORMATTING — 43

FORMATS — 46

STEP 8: EXPANDING THE SEARCH — 49

CATEGORIES — 53

STEP 9: TO THE MOON — 55

PRE-LAUNCH — 56
FREE PHASE — 61
SAVING A DEAD BOOK — 61

PROFITABLE AMAZON ADS — 63

KEYWORDS FOR ADS — 64
CAMPAIGN TYPES — 64
BUDGET AND BID — 65
CAMPAIGN BIDDING STRATEGY — 66
AD FORMAT — 66
PRODUCTS — 67
TARGETING — 67
LAUNCHING ADS — 67
MONITOR — 69
OUTSOURCING — 70

MORE PASSIVE INCOME — 73

LAUNCHING AN AUDIOBOOK — 76
EVEN MORE MONEY — 77
INGRAMSPARK — 77
GOOGLE PLAY & DRAFT 2 DIGITAL — 78
FINDAWAY VOICES & AUTHORS REPUBLIC — 79
TRANSLATIONS — 79
BUNDLES — 80

STANDING ON THE SHOULDERS OF GIANTS — 81

IDENTITY — 82
DESIGN — 82
SUPPORTING MATERIALS — 83

BUSINESS SETUP & TAX OPTIMIZATION STRATEGIES---87
Banking---88
Virtual assistants---88

CONCLUSION---91
Quality is what will make you stand out.---92

ABOUT ME---95

RESOURCES---99

OTHER BOOKS BY WILLIAM SWAIN---100

INTRODUCTION

Did you know that anyone can publish a book? It might seem like something exclusive reserved only for the celebrities, big brands or influencers. But publishing a book doesn't require a huge amount of money or even a deal with a big-name publisher. In fact, you can go solo and still make a huge impact. David Goggins is a retired navy seal who turned down traditional publishing deals and instead took the self-published route. This turned out to be a wise move because his compelling autobiography, a tale of overcoming the odds became a bestseller. Millions of dollars have gone to him which otherwise would have gone into the pockets of publishers.

We are now living in an age where people are thirsty for new content. More books are being consumed than ever before whilst content is becoming easier to produce. Barriers to entry which were previously held by the big-name publishers are being lowered. The power dynamic is shifting. With self-publishing the power is in your hands to publish the books you want, when you want and to earn as much as you want. Maybe you came here because you have a great idea for a book. But you feel lost because you don't have deals with traditional publishers. Or maybe you're an entrepreneur looking to make money online with a side hustle. Or maybe you tried self-publishing before but you didn't get many sales. However, you are still here.

I know how it feels. There was a time (well a few years) where I had tried so many ways to make money online. There was a time when I had no idea how to write and market my books. But I persisted and dove deep down into the rabbit hole of becoming a better publisher. Over the years through trial and error I have refined a nine-step system which has made me over $30,000 in one month. And half of that came from just one book! There was no big-name support, I worked just a few hours per week and invested around $1000.

Now I am going to share with you the nine steps in this book. Whether you're an author or entrepreneur I'll show you how to turn your ideas into successful self-published books. I promise to show you how to make sure your book is placed at the top of the pile helping you earn more money and success. I won't waste your time with confusing technical terms, nerdy stuff, or time-wasting activities. Neither will I show you how to spam sales with a ton of low quality or low content books. My system focuses on nine steps to produce high quality, sustainable business methods. Along with that I offer even more ways to optimize your business and leverage your books in the long term.

Whilst it's true that everything in this book can be found for free online. It's also true that such information will be all over the place and from various sources. In the end that way will leave you even more confused! Stop wasting time and follow my nine step system that won't require you to consume more books, videos or hop on a call. Everything you need to get started and succeed with self-publishing is right here. Follow the steps, read through them all and revisit them. Now without further ado let's get straight to the point with the exact steps you need to take.

And that first step begins on the next page.

THE MOST IMPORTANT STEP

We begin this book with keyword research which is the most important step of creating a bestselling book. Get it right and make big money. Rush it and you will get no sales. Now when it comes to keyword research it's all about finding profitable keywords which we could potentially publish a book on. We can then determine whether these books would be worthwhile to publish on by analyzing certain metrics. For authors with books written you need to understand what keywords will fit your book best. Essentially, we are looking for high demand and low competition. This is basic business fundamentals. Find where there are many customers wanting something with not many other competitors. Accomplishing this requires us to find the right keywords. Thankfully there are a few methods to help find them.

Brainstorm

Begin compiling your list of keywords by brainstorming keywords you think could make good book ideas. Write down at least twenty different keywords which you think would make great books. To help you come up with ideas visit bookstores or browse online.

Bookbeam

Book beam is a useful tool for not only finding keywords but also for checking their profitably. For just forty dollars per month you can utilize it to find potentially profitable keywords. Simply sign up and head over to the niche finder section. Keep things quite broad at first. Follow these steps.

1. Select self-published books so that you cut out all the established publishers who would be difficult to compete with. To find out if that is the case scroll down to the product details section and check "Publisher" where it should say "Independently published"
2. Select best seller rank from 10,000 to 200,000.
3. Select categories. Go through a few and create lists of potential keywords.

Now you will be presented with a list of books within the ranges and categories which you set. Click on some of those books and start to consider whether you could compete with them. Identify books without too many reviews and that look like they are self-published. Anything with over one thousand reviews disregard. Grind it out for a while until you find at least twenty potential keywords. To find the keyword simply look at the title or it should be obvious enough what the main theme of the book is.

https://bookbeam.io/

Category search

Go to www.amazon.com and visit the books section. Start browsing through various categories. Identify books with the potential to be self-published. The best categories to get involved in are as follows. Note that I have left out many categories because they will be too competitive for you to enter. Generally, I would say to go for anything within the following categories.

- Business and money
- Children's books
- Cookbooks
- Computers and technology
- Crafts, hobbies and home
- Foreign languages
- Fiction – this covers a broad range of genres such as science fiction, romance, thrillers and so on. If you do decide to go into fiction, realize that you will need to build a brand around it. Typically, people will want to see a face for a brand, and we can talk more about that later on in the brand building section.
- Health, fitness and dieting
- Self-help

- Sports and outdoors
- Travel

Metrics

Once you have some keyword ideas you will need to analyze their profitability. Start by looking at the first page of results on Amazon. Open at least four books on that page which look self-published, are using your keyword and are within the top 200,000 of results. Alternatively use the KDSPY Chrome extension to make the process more streamlined. When using KDSPY make sure you remove outliers from your lists. Those would be anything with a result that is way outside of the others. For example if most books on the list have a BSR of around 100,000 and you see one with 100,000,000 then remove it because otherwise it will adversely affect the results. The same applies for very low ranking or unrelated books. Record all of your data in a spreadsheet and across that spreadsheet create the following columns.

I have a copy of this on my website.
https://www.subscribepage.com/fortunepublishing

Average Best Seller Rank (BSR)

Essentially this indicates demand for a keyword. BSR can be found by clicking on a books page on Amazon and then scrolling down to the publisher information section. Tools such as Bookbeam and KDSPY also show you this metric. Ideally it should be from 10,000 to 200,000. More than that and things start to become too competitive. Less and it starts to become unprofitable.

Reviews

Aim to find keywords with books that have an average of under five hundred reviews. Realize that books with more reviews will be from very well-established authors and thus more difficult to compete with.

Competitors

The number of competitors can be found when searching for a keyword on Amazon. It will be displayed at the top left side of the page. Essentially this indicates the number of books published on that keyword. Anything over ten thousand competitors and things start to become too competitive. Realistically there are more and more books being published all the time so naturally this will always go up. Many of those books will be low quality books. Overall try to avoid crazy high numbers like anything over twenty thousand competitors.

Number of books published in the last 6 months

Here is an often-overlooked metric. How many books on the first page were published within the last six months? If you see anything over two books on the first page that have been published within the last six months, then be careful. Essentially that would indicate that many new publishers are continually entering the market. Ultimately this will saturate the market and make any success you do have short lived.

Audiobooks

Moving on we apply similar research for audiobooks. Head over to www.audible.com and search for your keyword. Analyze the results on the first page.

- We look at the number of competitors
    - Under 50 is good
    - 50 to 200 is ok
    - Over 200 is hard to compete
- We look at rank – we can use BSR tool or Bookbeam for this
    - Under 100,000 is good
    - 100,000 to 200,000 is ok
    - Over 200,000 would be hard to compete

Score

Now that we have analyzed all metrics, we can make a score. The score is based on the following.

- Potential of book on Amazon
    - How in demand it is (average BSR)
    - How much competition there is (number of books published)
- Potential of audiobook
    - How in demand it is (average BSR)
    - How much competition there is

(number of books published)
- Add the above together and divide by two. Score from 1 to 5.

Note: [Bookbeam](#) offers a scoring system based on competition and opportunity.

Add up the scores for both the book and audiobook. Ideally you want to go for an all-round book that is great to read and listen to. However, you might want to shoot just for audio or just for paperback versions. Sometimes for example you might want to create a book for marketing purposes. In that case you could disregard the audiobook metrics. Or vice versa. For example, you might want to create a book about breathing exercises which would be aimed at audio format.

[Here is my spreadsheet.](https://www.subscribepage.com/fortunepublishing)
https://www.subscribepage.com/fortunepublishing

STEP 2
OUTLINING

Once you have decided on a keyword it's time to create an outline which is what you will give to a writer. The more details the better an outcome you can influence. Conducting thorough research will help you to identify all of the elements and points of the keyword you're going to invest in. Now there is the option of paying for an outline and for around seventy five dollars you can hire someone to create a detailed outline for you. Just search on Fiverr for services offering this. Check the reviews and select a good one. For more experienced self-publishers who are looking to outsource their skills and focus on the bigger picture it is a great option. For beginners I would suggest working on the outline yourself so that you can fully understand what goes into a book every step of the way. As you grow you can outsource things but it's important to understand how it all works first which comes from grinding it out for yourself.

Outline steps

To begin your outline, create a document. I suggest using Google docs for this so that you can keep everything online. Next search your keyword on Amazon and identify your top four competitors. Ideally these should all be self-published. Make sure they are ranking within the top 200,000 best seller rank. This ensures they are selling and have some kind of track record. You can find this information next to the publisher details.

Start mining these four books for information to add to your outline. Open the books and copy over their table of contents. Summarize them into common elements and focus on identifying the key points. For now, don't worry about them being in any particular order because later your writing team can take care of that.

Next look through the reviews. Begin with one-star reviews. Look for the pain points of customers such as any complaints they have and so on. This will help you understand what to avoid or what to add. For example, maybe they complain about dry writing or missing certain things. Let your writer know about all of this. Next look at the five- and four-star reviews. Look for cool phrases or benefits people gained from the book. Some of these can be used in your outline and description later. Indeed, you might even find some useful headers.

Head over to YouTube and type in your keyword. Open up any videos that look relevant to your subject. Copy any titles or descriptions that you think are compelling and fit well. Do the same thing on Udemy where you can find some courses on your subject. Make note of their titles and descriptions. Add them to your outline. Finally check the first eight pages of search results on Google. Open up any decent looking pages of relevant information. Copy across any interesting or useful data to your outline. In your outline I suggest the following sections.

- Main keys
    - Add in your main keywords here
- Competition / title ideas
    - Add in the top four competitors here
- Research
    - Amazon books
    - Amazon reviews (look at 5 star and 1-star reviews)
    - Udemy
    - Youtube titles
    - Google first eight pages
- Titles
    - Add in potential titles here
- Headlines
    - Add in potential headlines here
- Ideal outcomes
    - Add in the ideal outcome's readers would achieve. For example – lose

weight, get rich, learn faster and so on.
- Objections
    - Add in the common objection's readers might have. For example – it takes too much time, is not suitable for my work life, frustrating and so on.
- Phrases
    - Add in common phrases here. For example – optimal health, make money online, quick, and easy to implement, etc..
- Facts
    - Add in any facts here.
- Questions
    - Add in any common questions here.
- Bullets
    - Add in anything that you could use as a bullet point here.

Creating the outline

Now that you have some basic notes and contents you can start to organize them. At the start of the outline create a short note to the writer letting them know that "we will work on this together". Inform them that you want this book to add value and that there are five key points the book must focus on.

1. Information
2. Focus
3. Organization

4. Flow
5. Enjoyable

Finally, let them know that they should avoid plagiarism and unnecessary filler writing. Restate and affirm that quality is paramount. Moving on here is an overview of recommended sections for an outline.

You can find my outline template here.
https://www.subscribepage.com/fortunepublishing

- Title
    - Add in your title here. For now, this can be just the keyword along with any other related keywords.
- Author
    - This would be your author's name. Research other competitors. For example, are they usually men or women? Or could you create a company?
- Word count
    - For word count I suggest at least twenty eight thousand words. This will allow you to price your book at an optimal price point on Audible.
- Target audience
    - Here you can add in age and gender. Maybe it's for adults, kids or for beginners and so on.
- Problem that leads the customer to purchase

this book
  - Use your earlier research to list any objections or complaints you have identified.
- Solution to that problem
  - Use your earlier research to list any positive reviews or ideal outcomes you have identified.
- Summary and purpose of the book
  - Summarize the main purpose of the book using your research.
- Top competitive titles
  - Add in the top competitors here.

Introduction

Moving on we have the chapter outlines. Begin with an introduction which can be about two thousand words. Use this basic seven step introduction formula.

1. Identify and state the problem
   a. Use your earlier research here.
2. Present the solution
   a. Use your earlier research here.
3. Assert credibility
   a. Have your writer or you create some background information about the author.
4. Show them the benefits
   a. Use your earlier research here.
5. Give them proof

a.   Use your earlier research here.
6. Make a promise
   a.   Have your writer create something here
7. Create a sense of urgency and a call to action
   a.   Have your writer create something here

Body chapters

Next, we have the body chapters which should deliver on any promises made in the introduction. For a twenty-eight-thousand-word book they would be about two to four thousand words per chapter. Use your research and gather the contents of competing books here. Now don't worry about them being in any particular order. Simply let your writer know that they are basic notes. If you want to spend more time organizing, go ahead. Otherwise have someone else take care of this for you.

Conclusion

Finally, we have the conclusion which should give a good closure to the book. Make it at least one thousand words. In conclusion the writer should summarize the main topics, restate the most important message, state how the promises of the introduction were delivered and add anything else you want the reader to take from the book.

Resources page

Make sure your writer creates a resources page in APA format with all the resources that they used to write this book.

Here is a free APA citation generator they can use: https://www.scribbr.com/apa-citation-generator/

Most common reasons for bad reviews

Lastly create a section at the end of the outline with a list of reasons for bad reviews. We want to avoid bad reviews. Therefore, it's important to understand why other competing books might have received bad reviews. Use your earlier research to list the top reasons why people left bad reviews on similar books.

STEP 3
PROFESSIONAL BOOK WRITING

Now that you have created a solid outline it's time to make an order to have it turned into a book. For this step I suggest spending as much as you can afford on a writing company or freelancer. Most of the writing companies are similar nowadays. But you should always be responsible for keeping a close eye on your project. Don't just give it over to them and assume they will do an amazing job. It's on you to monitor it.

For those of you who are on a budget you can alternatively write the book yourself. One way to easily achieve this is to set yourself a goal to write one thousand words a day. Keep a chart of it to stay motivated. Work in twenty-five-minute chunks every day and in just one month you will have a book! Writing the book yourself can be a great experience. Especially if you're curious or knowledgeable about a subject. Writing about it forges your knowledge further. Again, it's a great exercise in learning, discipline and becoming more familiar with the publishing process. And if that's not for you then check out some of the writing services below.

The Urban Writers

The Urban Writers are the largest writing company right now. They are well experienced and have a big enough team to handle many orders. Beyond writing they also offer translations, narration, outlines and much more. Make use of the code "JUAN" for a five percent discount.

TUW works by creating a project and selecting any add on such as bundle options with a fully delivered book and descriptions, illustrations, outlines and even covers. Otherwise you can just go for a writing package only where you get to choose your own writer and editor. Currently they offer various fiction and non-fiction packages.

- Fiction = $3.69 per 100 words ($1107 for a 30k book)
- Finance and technology = $3.69 per 100 words ($1350 for a 30k book)
- Premium = $3.69 per 100 words ($1107 for a 30k book) – highest performers. Includes up to twenty images.
- Top = $3.49 per 100 words ($1047 for a 30k book) – writers who produce high quality work. Includes up to 10 images.

- Urban = $3.19 per 100 words ($957 for a 30k book) – up and coming talent.
- Rising = $2.60 per 100 words ($780 for a 30k book) – new starters with The Urban Writers.

The Writing Summit

The Writing Summit is a team of authors who have partnered with high-quality writers, and editors. According to them they have a large team with a diversified knowledge of publishing platforms and content marketing. Currently they offer three packages.

Package 1
- Top writer
- 35 days delivery time (30k words)
- Proofread
- Edited
- eBook formatting
- Plagiarism checks
- Revision
- $2.99 per 100 words ($897 for a 30k word book)

Package 2
- Intermediate Writer
- 35 days delivery time (30k words)
- Lightly Edited
- eBook Formatting
- Plagiarism checks

- $2.75 per 100 words ($825 for a 30k word book)

Package 3
- Budget Writer
- 35 days delivery time (30k words)
- No Revisions
- eBook Formatting
- Plagiarism checks
- $2.15 per 100 words ($645 for a 30k word book)

Best only for simple content and basic topics.

Hot Ghost Writer

Personally, I haven't used Hot Ghostwriter, so I don't know how good they are. However they claim to be "The self-publisher's official book ghostwriting service." For a standard nonfiction book of thirty thousand words their price is $1560. Various other parts can be added on as well such as narration for audiobooks, outlines and so on.

Upwork

Upwork is a website where you can directly find writers. Simply post a job offer and then start interviewing candidates. This process does take more time, but it can be a cheaper option with more control in your hands. However, you will need to be careful as there are many writers who plagiarize there. Be sure you video interview them and create a writing test before hiring them. This will cut out any people who might be faking their identity or credentials. When they deliver your project make sure you run in it through plagiarism scanners and check it hasn't been published before.

Fiverr

Fiverr is similar to Upwork in that you will be directly in contact with writers. Again, you will have to work with due diligence to ensure you have a legitimate writer. You can also check through their reviews and customer experiences. Search through the writer section on Fiverr to identify any that have experience in your niche. Personally, I haven't used Fiverr for writing projects. But I have heard if you shop around, you can get a good deal. Usually, I go with writing companies because they already have verified the writer's quality.

https://www.fiverr.com/

Checking your project

Once your project has been delivered, run it through plagiarism scanners. I recommend buying credits on Copyscape. Run the finished book through there at about two thousand words per time. This will compare it against published books and online content for anything similar. Now just be aware that the scanning process will pull up quotes and references. However, if those have been properly referenced, then it is fine. What you don't want is clearly copied content that has not been referenced at all because this will get you in trouble. Should you identify any plagiarized content, talk with your writer. Have them revise the work or in the worst case refund you.

In addition to Copyscape scans perform a quick search on Amazon to make sure the book has not been published already. Rarely does this happen but you never know, and you don't want it to happen to you. Search your keyword and check for any books published within the last ninety days. Make sure none of those contain content from your book.

Finally read through your book to make sure it is good and that you're happy with it. Read through it all to make sure you fully understand the content. Additionally, you can copy sections of it for your description. Find parts you can use as bullet points, headings, and for good overviews. Typically, the introduction and conclusion will contain some great content for the description. Once you are happy with the book's content it's time to move onto the next steps of self-publishing.

STEP 4
TITLES THAT SELL

When your book has been written it's time to work on creating a bestselling title. I recommend waiting until the book is written because it allows you to gather content from it which will help you to create the best fitting title. A well written title will help your book sell through being optimized for search ranking and briefly explaining what it is about. Many self-publishers make the mistake of either being too vague, keyword stuffing or creating unsuitable titles. Craft a title with a good balance of keywords whilst making sense to read. Furthermore, remember to be specific and relevant.

So, what goes into a great title? First of all it's good practice to put your main keyword at the start of the title. For best results that would come before a colon. For example,

- Make Money Online: How to Make Passive Income

- Fat Loss Diet: Lose Weight
- Cryptocurrency for Beginners: Start your Bitcoin Journey

When it comes to creating a title there are certain things you will need to avoid.

- The title should not exceed two hundred characters.
- The title should match the cover title.
- There should be no claims of bestseller or rank.
- There should be no claim of deals or discounts.
- There should be no keyword stuffing whereby you put too many keywords into the title.
- There should be no trademarks. Check here for any active trademarks:
  https://www.uspto.gov/trademarks/search

Now that we have covered what not to do let's examine what goes into creating a great title. A great title should be specific and bold. Imagine someone trying to sell your book. What would they say about specifically? Ideally you should tell potential readers exactly what your book is about. Let's take a look at how to effectively do that.

List the benefits

A title that sells is effective at listing the benefits it might offer to readers. What are some of the benefits that reading your book might offer? Let's imagine it was a ketogenic book. Some benefits could be for example to lose weight, have more energy and save time on meal plans. Go ahead and list as many benefits as you can come up with. Get creative and use your imagination to list all of the potential benefits from the biggest to the smallest. Next highlight those that are the biggest attention grabbers.

With those benefits listed you can now begin to expand on them. Create sentences that highlight those benefits and speak to any potential pain points. Be subtle and spell out how you will offer benefits and solutions. Don't worry about writing something perfect for now just write and let it flow. We can revise and perfect things later. Set a timer to write as many benefits as possible within five minutes and then pick out the best three. Let's look at how to do that using our earlier example.

- Lose weight even if you gained too much at Christmas.
- Lose weight even if you're older.
- Lose weight even if you struggle to stick to diets.
- Have more energy even if you're lazy.
- Have more energy even if you hate exercise.
- Have more energy even if you struggle to get out of bed.
- Save time on meal plans even if you don't cook.
- Save time on meal plans even if you work

everyday.
- Save time on meal plans even if you hate cooking.

Next choose the titles which you would like to refine. Focus on making them more specific, eye-catching and bold. Once you have a good title you will want to make sure it appears in search results whilst still being readable.

Bad title example 1
Keto Diet: Lose Weight, Have More Energy, Save Time on Meal Plans, Recipes, Fitness, 6 Pack, Diet and Health

The above is very keyword stuffed and looks unrelatable for a human being.

Bad title example 2
Keto Diet: Try this new way out to lose weight and feel like you're young once again. It really works, trust me.

The above is more relatable but it's quite weak and doesn't really target audiences well. Plus, it lacks keywords in the title which could potentially bring in more sales.

Good title example
Keto Diet: Lose Weight, Have More Energy & Save Time on Meal Plans - Even if You Are Older, Hate Exercise and Struggle with Diets.

The above title is a great fit because it lists the

benefits and speaks directly to some common objections of the target audience. Those are probably thirties and up folks so they will often have those kinds of objections. Continue to develop your title with some of these methods.

- Keywords
- Sample your story
- Find well known phrases
- Try emotional trigger words

Keywords

Take the top three to five keywords from your keyword research and add them into the title in a readable way that makes sense. This should be appealing to your readers whilst also helping your book to rank for more keywords. Here are some examples.

- Keywords: ketogenic diet, lose weight, healthy body, lifestyle,
- How to make them into a title
    - Ketogenic Diet: The beginners guide to lose weight and gain a healthy body with this simple lifestyle change.

The above example makes sense. It isn't just some keywords stuffed together. Whilst it also covers all our keywords in a neat sentence that makes sense. If you need to find more keywords, then head over to "Step 8" in this book.

Sample your story

Sampling a part of your story works best for fiction. Often this is a tricky one to create a title for. When the writer delivers your book, have a look through it for potential title ideas. Maybe you could use character names or something about the setting. Maybe you could use something about the time or something from the main events or themes. Perhaps you could find one great line from the book.

Common phrases

During your research you might notice common phrases coming up again and again. Make a note of those because they could work well in your title. Again, remember to never use trademarks.

Emotional trigger words

There are certain words that are good at conveying emotions. These tend to stick in readers' minds much more than plain words do. Ultimately that can help you with conversions. Simply changing and tweaking a few words can make a huge difference. Look at your title ideas. Switch out any weak words with more powerful ones. Make use of a thesaurus. For example,

- Amazing - becomes mind blowing.
- Cool - becomes awe inspiring.
- Big - becomes ginormous.
- Powerful - becomes rocket powered.

Be creative and get going! Remember to start with listing the benefits and then work on developing a great title. Readers should know exactly what they are buying. Remember to never mislead people or click bait them. To summarize your title should be.

- Enticing / offers significant value
- Intriguing
- Specific
- Relevant
- Search engine friendly

Once you're happy with the title, move on to the next step.

STEP 5
BEST SELLING DESCRIPTION

Writing a description for your book is a very important part of the self-publishing process that should never be rushed. The description is what appears on a books sales page. The purpose of it is to effectively convey the book's purpose and value to potential customers. Again, this is a step that can be outsourced. [Fiverr](#) has many great services for this. However, for beginners it's a good idea to get familiar with this process because copywriting is a very valuable skill to learn. Fortunately, I have made the process quite easy for you. During your research, you should have found lots of information which you can use here.

Formats

Look at the descriptions of your top four competitors. How have they written them? Do most begin with a heading? Do they ask certain questions? Do they talk about certain issues? How do they list benefits? How do they close the description?

Investigate your competitors to fully understand the niche you're going into. Then you can start to formulate your own description. Use the notes you collected earlier along with any information from your completed book. Here are some elements that go into writing a bestselling description.

Headline

Most headlines are too salesy and difficult to believe. A great headline should create vision, be intriguing yet also be believable. Let's look at some examples.

- Make money online fast with this system (this sounds like typical internet hype and most people are unlikely to buy it)
- Make money online in seven different ways (this is a little bit better because it gets more specific and is more believable, although it's still a little dry)
- Seven realistic ways to make money online in 2023 and beyond (this is much more attractive to read whilst also being specific, believable, and relevant)

Analyze your notes from earlier and find elements you could turn into headlines. Try adding words such as "proven, realistic, new", and so on. Adding the year is great for creating more relevance. Furthermore, numbers are awesome for being specific. Let's look at one more example in the weight loss niche.

- How to lose weight with this guide (this is way too generic and could be anything, it's not enticing at all)
- How to lose weight and fit into your new jeans (this is a cool title and speaks to a pain point of people trying to lose weight, you can almost visualize it)
- How to easily lose weight and fit into your new jeans without crash diets or grueling workouts (even better because speaks to the many pain points and common customer objections)

<u>For all of the other elements that go into a best selling description check out my free template.</u>
https://www.subscribepage.com/fortunepublishing

Finally, be aware of some things to avoid. Amazon doesn't want you to mislead customers or sell them a bad book. If they don't like your book description, then they might not allow you to run ads to it. Always stick to their terms and conditions.

https://advertising.amazon.com/resources/ad-policy/book-ads

Keep revising your description. Again it's powerful so make use of formatting with some areas in **bold**, *italic* or <u>underlined</u> to **emphasize points** and so on. The final description should fit neatly onto one page. I know it's a lot to take in but spend the time here.

Copywriting is a valuable skill to learn that will not only help you sell books but also help you with marketing campaigns and much more.

STEP 6
CREATING A COVER

Now that you have your incredible title written it's time to create a cover. Remember that the title must match what you put on the cover as well as the back end metadata. When it comes to creating a cover, you can either do it yourself using design tools such as Canva or hire someone to do it. Unless you have a design background or a tight budget, I would suggest hiring a professional. For as little as $7.50 you can get a professional quality cover. Don't underestimate the price, one of my books with a $7.50 cover made me over fifteen thousand dollars in one month!

Finding designers

My go-to resource for cover designers has always been Fiverr. There are other services such as those from ghost-writing companies. Just realize those are usually more expensive and perhaps offer less revisions. With Fiverr you can search on their platform for cover designers. Pick a few that you like the look of and that are within your budget. Don't assume that higher prices mean better quality. Again, I have made amazing sales with $7.50 covers. When you search for designers make sure they have good reviews, offer revisions, create great quality, high-definition images and deliver on time. Cover designers will often require a basic specification. Of course, they will want your title and author name. Plus, beyond that they will want to know a few things. Consider the following:

- Standing out – search your top four competitors. What styles are they using? How can you stand out? Maybe it's color or intrigue. For example, they use black backgrounds, so you use white. Or maybe you use an intriguing image such as a mysterious box, a person and so on.
- Color – what are your preferences for color? What colors would stand out?
- Image – have a search on https://depositphotos.com/ for images. Look at their vectors, illustrations, and images for ideas. Choose a few and send them to your designers. Most designers will have an account here.
- Text – what style of text would you prefer? What arrangement? Maybe you would like a text only book?
- Brand – are you creating a brand? If so, notify your designer and create any other books in

that brand using similar styles.

Consider all of the above and send your specifications to your designer. Try a few different designs and then select the one you like the best. If you can't decide then choose your top three and share them in publishing groups or with your friends. Later on you can always change the cover. Ultimately such a change could increase your sales.

Back cover

For the paperback and hardcover versions, you will need a back cover. This should be delivered in PDF format sized as your book should be. Usually for a book of up to thirty thousand words I would suggest 8 x 5 size. Customers often complain when a book is too thin. Such a sizing will make your book seem much thicker and less like a pamphlet. For larger content books that are above thirty thousand words go with a 6 x 9 size. Most cover designers will be able to provide a back cover design for you. On the back cover I suggest keeping the same color scheme and simply adding your sales description on there. If you want to you can add a hyperlink to your website or even an author image if it's relevant.

Audible cover

Finally, you will want your cover to be formatted for Audible. Their requirement is 2400 x 2400 pixels. Now don't just stretch your cover because it looks cheap and amateur to do this. Ask your cover designer to provide you with this specific size also and tip them for it. Make sure it all looks good and then you're ready to go.

STEP 7
BEAUTIFUL FORMATTING

Now that you have your book completed along with the title and cover it's time to start formatting it. When it comes to formatting the book itself the task can be quite cumbersome and technical. If you're patient enough or have a tight budget, then learn the steps and try it for yourself. YouTube has plenty of tutorials. Otherwise hire a professional to format for you. Fiverr has loads of options for you to choose from. From about thirty dollars you can easily get all formats delivered. Begin with gathering all the elements which you are going to include inside of the book. Here is a list of what to include.

Title page

The first page is the title page. Here you would include the title in big bold letters, then a line and the subtitle under that. At the bottom of this page add your author's name. Then add two blank pages. This will create a neat space for the next page to start on an odd number so that when printed the book is always starting on the first left hand page.

Headers and footers

I suggest you have the book title and the author's name in the headers. Set these to alternate on each page. In the footer put page numbers. Skip these on the title page.

Copyright page

Add in a standard copyright page containing your author's name and the year it was published at the top. See the start of this book for example. It should all fit neatly onto one page. Add two blank pages after this.

Lead magnet

Add your lead magnet in here. Create a hyperlink and write the link out for paperback and hardcover editions. Add a blank page after so that the next page starts on the left (odd page number).

Contents

Add in your table of contents next. Use hyperlinks and page numbers. Add a blank page or two after so that the next page starts on the left (odd page number).

Introduction

Write in your introduction here.

The book itself

Write in your book itself here. End with a note

which encourages reviews.

References

At the end of your book, you can add in any references. Be sure to add the citations in the relevant parts of the book as well. Usually that's something like this (Williams, 1982). That will relate to the reference at the end. I suggest you use an APA tool for compiling references. Whether you are quoting a book, website, or anything else it makes the citation and reference in correct formats.

https://www.scribbr.com/apa-citation-generator/

Lead magnet

Add your lead magnet in again here.

Other books by

Write in links to any other books you have along with a short summary of them. Use the book blurbs. In addition, add any links to your website or social media channels. Make use of online QR code generators to create scannable links. Make sure you also write the links out for paperback versions of the book.

Use my template for book
https://www.subscribepage.com/fortunepublishing

Fonts

There are certain fonts which work perfectly for

books. When choosing a font make sure it is easy to read. Avoid anything too big or too small. Include spacing so it's not all jammed together. Generally, you can use the same font for the eBook and hard copy versions. Here are some of the best fonts to use.

- Bookerly
- Bitter HT
- Georgia
- ChareInk
- Avenir Next
- Literata
- Raleway
- Linux Biolinum
- Palatino
- Lora

Formats

eBook

For the eBook version of your book, you will need it delivered in PDF, eBook, mobi and docx formats. I suggest Microsoft Word for all formatting. They offer a monthly subscription for around ten dollars. Otherwise try Kindle Create which is a free Amazon tool for formatting. It's less flexible but easily delivers quality results. Along with the eBook you will need your cover. Make sure that the title matches all of the book data.

Paperback

Paperbacks come in several different sizes and styles. Generally, for anything up to thirty thousand words I suggest a 5 x 8 size. For smaller content books it makes them seem much thicker and is kind of an industry standard size. As I mentioned earlier, sometimes customers complain about book thickness, so this size is good to go with. For bigger content books go with 6 x 9 size. Again, Microsoft Word is an excellent formatting tool. Amazon offers download templates for the various sizes and then you can simply adjust your content to fit into those.

For the paperback version you will also need to format a cover. Kindle has PDF templates for this. Download the relevant size and then open it up in [Canva](#) (great tool for publishing and your team can use it). Add in your front cover to fit within the recommended lines. Then create a back cover and add your blurb text to this. Make sure the color scheme makes sense and if you want to add any links or author pictures.

Hardcover

The hardcover is similar to the paperback but just a few inches different and you will also need a spine on there. The spine is the thin area on the side of the book. Write in the title and author name here. When you upload paperback and hardcover to Kindle you will have the chance to preview them and make adjustments if necessary.

STEP 8
EXPANDING THE SEARCH

Whilst your book is being written you can work on some back-end tasks. At this point you should have a handful of keywords. Now you will need to add those with more related keywords. When you publish a book, you can add up to seven supporting keywords in the back end metadata. These will be linked to your book and help it to rank for even more keywords. In addition, you will need some keywords for your advertising campaigns. Let's look at all the steps to collecting more keywords in detail.

Brainstorm

There are several ways you can find more keywords. To begin with I suggest you brainstorm anything that might be associated with your main keyword. Also look at your top four competitors. Do they have any keywords in their titles or descriptions? From your earlier research can you identify any more keywords?

An excellent tool for initial keyword research is [KDSPY](#) which comes as a Google Chrome extension. Once you have it installed head over to Amazon and search for your main keyword. Open up [KDSPY](#) and then click on the "word cloud" link. List down any keywords that are related. Ignore common things such as "they, you or most" and so on. Bookbeam is another great tool for keyword research. Make use of their options.

Auto-populate

By now you should have around ten to twenty extra keywords. Expand upon those with longer tail keywords and variations of them. Head over to Amazon and select the search bar to "books". Slowly type your different keywords into the search bar. As you type them in, notice that the search bar will auto populate with some results. Make a note of those.

Google and YouTube

Search your keywords on Google and YouTube. Note down any keywords that are relevant. Page, video titles and descriptions are the best place to find them. On YouTube you can also look at the metadata to see the exact keywords used. To do that use Google Chrome. Select the following – view – developer - source and then click control find "keywords". Note down any relevant keywords.

KDP Rocket

KDP Rocket is an essential tool for the self-publisher. For around $99 you get a lifetime purchase. Use it to find tons of keywords, categories, and for competitor research. Take your growing keyword list and open up KDP Rocket. Again, I highly recommend you use this essential research tool. There are others out there but for my strategy I suggest KDP Rocket. Inside of the tool open the "Keyword Search" tab. Here you can enter each of your keywords and then download the data to add to your list. Once complete you should have a pretty big list of keywords. It's time to narrow that list down.

Refinement

On your main list create a column next to it called "relevance". Now simply go down the list and mark an "X" next to any keyword you think is relevant. If you see many keywords that start the same then just choose the first one. For example,

- Investing crypto for beginners
- Investing crypto on a budget
- Investing crypto for moms

Choose the first part, "Investing crypto". Once you have selected all keywords that are relevant, organize the list to show only those relevant ones. These will be used for our advertising campaigns and for the top seven keywords.

Top seven keywords

The top seven keywords are what we enter into the back end meta-data of a book on Amazon. I suggest splitting these into two sets. Four can be for single keywords. Three can be a few keywords linked together. Amazon allows about fifty characters in the keyword box so make use of that. So, what should you put in these seven boxes?

First, create a new column called "high relevance" then put an "X" next to anything which is highly relevant. Next add your title to the document so you can see any keywords that you already have in the title. We won't need to use any keywords that are already in the title. And if you haven't created your title yet, then take a moment to go over that in the next chapter using some of these high relevance keywords. Once you have a title and high relevance keywords available you can start selecting keywords to use in the seven boxes. Take all those high relevance keywords and remove any that are in the title. Try combining some to use in three of the boxes.

Let's look at an example of how to do this with three different keywords.

- For beginners
- Stock trading
- Crypto

Since the above keywords are related you could

combine them. For example, they could go in as, "stock trading, crypto for beginners". People would usually search them in one of those ways and Amazon will recognize that. Apply this method for three of your seven boxes. For the remaining four slots, select single keywords that have high demand and low competition. Do a quick search on those metrics using the keyword research steps and then you will have all of your boxes all filled.

Categories

When you first publish a book, you can add it to two categories. KDP Rocket has a great research tool for finding categories. Use it to find at least ten categories for the eBook and paperback versions. For the main two categories choose categories which require the least number of sales to rank as number one within that category. This will help you to get a bestseller badge. Later, you can add more categories by contacting Amazon support. Just click the help section of Amazon and navigate to add more categories. Then you can simply send them the additional categories.

STEP 9
TO THE MOON

With your book beautifully delivered and ready to go we are now ready to initiate the launch sequence, to the moon! For a copy of the exact template I use for my launch sequence follow the link below.

[My launch document](https://www.subscribepage.com/fortunepublishing)
https://www.subscribepage.com/fortunepublishing

There are several steps to successfully launching a book. Follow them to guarantee your success. My launch strategy is divided into three steps: pre-launch, free promo, and post launch. Carefully go through each one and you will be more guaranteed to succeed. Yes it can seem daunting and a lot of investment both financially and in time, but it will be worth it in the long run. Just like many other businesses this one will likely be in the red for a while but in the long term it can become lucratively profitable. Keep that in mind. Books have a honeymoon period where they are favored by Amazon. Usually that's the first two to three weeks. Optimize this period as much as possible so that your book can rank better and become favored by the Amazon algorithm.

Pre-Launch

Upload for pre order

Upload your eBook to KDP as an epub file. Fill in all the boxes with your information. Then set it for pre-order one week in the future. This will give you plenty of time to promote your book to any promo sites and to your subscribers. It will also give you time to adjust in case of any errors with your formatting or designs and so on. For the paperback and hardcover upload, then once the eBook is live. Amazon doesn't allow pre-orders for these so there is no point uploading them until the eBook is live. I like to set my releases for Mondays because then I can work on them all together.

When it comes to pricing in the beginning, we want to gain as much exposure as possible. A lower price can help us to achieve that. Again, at the start of a book's life don't worry about profitability. Later you can increase prices. Here are the initial price points I recommend.

- eBook: $3.99
- Paperback: $9.99 (unless it's a bigger book then you will need to price it higher for a base profit)
- Hardcover: $19.99 and up. We won't run ads

to our hardcover edition so price this as high as you like.

When you see pricing for other regions, round them up to the next nearest .99. Once you have uploaded the book, wait for approval on all formats and then move on to the next steps.

Add categories

Along with the two main categories we can add up to eight more for all editions of the book. Ranking in additional categories will help you to gain more bestseller badges. Through choosing smaller categories we can become a big fish in a small pond. To add those categories simply take your list of extra categories and head over to the link below and fill out the form.

https://author.amazon.com/en_US/contact

Book promotion sites

Book promotion sites will help your book to gain more buys, reviews, and downloads during the free promotion. I know it can be expensive using them all but give it a shot. Set your book promotion on these to match your KDP Select date (more on that later). This date would be one day after your book goes live and will last for five days. Here are some book promotion sites which I suggest.

- Book Sprout
- Book Sirens
- Fiverr

- Pubby

Book Funnel

Book funnel is an awesome website for building landing pages to your book. Send potential customers here from your lists or email marketing campaigns. Use a book funnel to create a landing page where they can download an advanced copy of your book. Encourage them to leave a rating or review on Amazon. They don't need to buy the book to do that. Difference between that and buying the book is that their review won't be verified. But it all helps.

https://dashboard.bookfunnel.com/

Four to six emails

If you have an email list for your brand, then I suggest writing four to six emails to them. Now if you don't have an email list then don't worry because it will eventually come from your books. Write a chain of emails to send after your book is live and leave a few days in between each email. Begin the first emails with promoting your book to be live and free on KDP Select. Make use of the blurb for headers and content of the emails. Send them to your funnel link and to where they can review the book. Request the reviews by a specific date. Around one month after the book is live should give them plenty of time. Remind them of reviewing your book again in the last two emails.

Email header:

> *Use something from the blurb or the book title.*

Content:

> *Welcome,*
>
>> *This week is a new FREE book launch, "book title here"*
>>
>> *(Add in something from the blurb here)*
>>
>> *Click here to download your FREE Copy*
>>
>> *(Add the link to the funnel here)*
>>
>> *And here is the book on Amazon*
>>
>> *(Add the link to the book on Amazon here)*
>>
>> *We would appreciate your review on Amazon on by "enter one month after live date"*
>>
>>> *Best regards,*
>>>
>>> *Author name*
>>>
>>> *Author website*

Website

If you have a website, post up the book and the links to buy it on Amazon. In addition, your website should have a blog. Post the emails as blog articles.

Social Media

If you have any social media channels, post the book and links to it on Amazon. Schedule posts the same as the emails.

Promo Video

Create a short promo video of your book. Make use of some free AI speech tools along with images or similar videos related to your book content. Use the blurb for the voice. Post this on your social media channels.

A + Content

A+ content is a recent addition to KDP and it's one you should take advantage of. Here you can add supporting images or videos that will appear near the bottom of your book's sales page. All of this can help the book to sell more copies. For sure you should make use of it to maximize sales. Work with a designer to create some images of your book conveying the key points and advantages. Make use of your description for this. Go ahead and research what your competitors are doing, then try and do something better!

Check it all looks good

Double check your sales page looks good on Amazon. Make sure the blurb looks well formatted. Make sure your cover and formatting look amazing. Once you're happy with how everything looks then move on to the next step.

For these steps:

[My launch document](https://www.subscribepage.com/fortunepublishing)
https://www.subscribepage.com/fortunepublishing

Free Phase

Post Promotion Period & Metrics

For these steps

[My launch document](https://www.subscribepage.com/fortunepublishing)
https://www.subscribepage.com/fortunepublishing

Saving a dead book

Realize in the beginning your books won't be profitable. Now if you find that after four weeks your book is just not making any money then analyze whether you need to change cover, description and so on. Get creative, try a different cover, a different blurb, or different keywords. Add more keywords to your ads. Now if that still doesn't work after six weeks, then cut your losses and move on. Even for the most experienced self-publishers we can still run into dead end books sometimes. Algorithms change, competitors come into the market along with many other variables. This is business. Don't get too attached to it. We can always repurpose it as a bundle or sell it on other platforms. If the ship is sinking, swim away from it to better lands.

Ok! Now we have gone through the nine steps of releasing your book. Congratulations, your book should now be live. It's now time to look at some excellent ways to optimize it and to gain even more revenue. Are you ready?

PROFITABLE AMAZON ADS

Amazon offers the opportunity to run adverts to your books in the USA, U.K, Canada, Germany, Australia, France, Germany, and Italy. For success on Amazon, they are essential. Unless you are uploading hundreds of books and trying to build multiple streams of organic sales then Amazon ads is the way to go. My strategy is producing high quality books promoted with profitable advertising and marketing campaigns.

To run Amazon adverts you will need a credit card to spend on the campaigns. Don't worry though because you can set limits and ultimately control how much you want to spend. With a good book in a decent niche, you can easily make profitable advertising campaigns. Again realize that at the start you will not be profitable. I know it can be stressful to see money going out and to not get an instant return on it. But this is a business which is a slow play. Every business requires money upfront and rarely do they make it back immediately. Investing at the start will help you to attain a good rank and later you can start to make it highly profitable. Play the game slowly and get rich in the long run.

Keywords for ads

For ad campaigns you will need around thirty keywords. High relevance keywords and those in the title will be what we use as our primary data. Other less relevant keywords can be used later on in the launch phase of our books to help them rank in more ways.

Campaign types

Sponsored product ads are going to be the main type of ad we use. Sponsored brands and lock ads are more for developed and established brands. There are three different types of adverts available. For a new book make use of all three types.

- Manual
    - This is coming from your list of keywords. Add those in as exact, phrase and broad. For anything less specific you can add them in as broad later. At the top you will need to select a manual to create this type of ad.
- Automatic
    - This is based on what Amazon thinks is the best for your book. Automatic ads work well in the early stages to gather data. Later, you can take data from them to other campaigns and

eventually turn them off. At the top you will need to select automatic to create this type of ad.
- Product
  - This is a collection of similar book ASINs and categories relevant to your book which you can bid on. When someone looks at those categories or similar books your book will appear. At the top you will need to select manual and then a product to create this type of ad.

Budget and bid

Budget

The budget of an advertising campaign is a tool used to set a limit for how much that campaign will spend per day. To begin with I suggest setting it at $7. As your ad becomes more profitable, increase it. If it becomes unprofitable then decrease it.

Bid

Bid relates to how much you choose to bid for a keyword. To begin with I recommend you set it at $0.40 cents. If your ads appear to not go live after a few days, relaunch them or check if they have been blocked. Sometimes Amazon might have issues with misleading descriptions or covers that need to be changed.

Campaign bidding strategy

Here you can choose how you want to pay for clicks on your ads. Check one of the following.

Dynamic bids - down only

This will lower your bids when your advert might not lead to a sale. Use this in the beginning.

Dynamic bids - up and down

This will raise your bids when your advert might lead to a sale and lower bids when it might not. Use this when you have narrowed down what keywords are converting.

Fixed bids

This will use an exact bid which won't change. Use this if you want to be very specific with how much you're willing to spend. Not recommended.

Adjust bids by placement (replaces Bid+)

Along with bidding strategy you have the option to increase bids by up to 900%. This is a great feature to help you rank. You can even adjust this separately for products and keywords. In the beginning set it to 200% and increase if you need to rank more. Later you can reduce this as reviews come in and your book ranks.

Ad Format

Here you can choose to use custom or standard ad text. I suggest you just go with standard unless you want to highlight something specific about your book in the advert.

Products

Type in the ASIN of the book which you want to run ads to.

Targeting

At this point you can start entering and setting bids for things. As I mentioned earlier it's good to begin with bids of $0.40 cents.

Match types

Match types allow you to fine tune your customer search terms.

- Broad: Contains all the keywords in any order and includes related, plurals and variations of keywords.
- Phrase: Containing the exact phrase or sequence of keywords.
- Exact: An exact match of the keyword or a sequence of keywords.

Launching ads

Here is the template I use to set up ad campaigns for new books.

- Launch date
  - Note the date the ads need to go live.
- Region
  - Note which regions to create ads in.

Begin with ads in the USA, UK, Australia and Canada. Later, if it goes well, consider other regions such as Germany, France, Spain and Italy. For those other regions you will need to translate the keywords.

- Title
    - The book title.
- Paperback or eBook
    - Begin with a paperback. After a few weeks if your book is doing well consider eBook ads.
- Keywords
    - Note the keyword tab or list you will use.
- Daily budget
    - Start at $7.
- Campaign bidding strategy
    - Begin with dynamic bids down only. Later on as you remove keywords you can focus in and change to up down.
- Adjust bids by placement
    - Begin with + 200%. Later if you need to rank more than increase this or decrease as you rank. For $0.40 cents that would go to about $1.60 per click.
- Type:
    - Automatic at $0.40 bids.
    - Manual at $0.40 bids. Take main

keywords and use broad, phrase, exact. Later add less specific broad keywords.
- Product at $0.40 bids. Use relevant ASINs and categories.

Monitor

Within three days you should start to see results. If there are no results then relaunch the ad. However only relaunch it if there are no ads giving results for that ad style. For example, if a category ad is already producing results (sales) then do not relaunch another category ad. Try to make sure there are not too many ad sets. Ultimately the goal of ads is to get the best results with the least amount of clicks. Each week you will need to check in on your ads. Use this step-by-step guide.

- Set date range to be last seven days
  - Go through each group one by one.
  - Identify any ads with many clicks and no sales or high ACOS (above %40)
    - Turn off any bad keywords (high ACOS or over 15 clicks and no sale)
    - Add them to negative keywords
- If there is less data, then set the date range to be the last 30 days or 90 days.
  - Repeat the same steps as above.
- Identify any campaigns with many orders.
  - Add whatever converted into more

exact, phrase and broad keywords at $.40 cent bids
- o Do the same with automatic ads but put them into manual ads.

Keep an eye on your ads but don't be checking on them every day. Understand that the algorithm lags so give it time. Ranges of 7 days, 30 days and year to date will give you a good analysis to make decisions from. (Amazon AMS)

Negative keyword targeting

As you gather more data you will notice some keywords generate many clicks but produce zero sales. This is bad. Make sure those keywords don't continue to spend on your ads by adding them to negative keyword targeting. Essentially this will stop them getting clicked for your ads and thereby make your ads more profitable.

Outsourcing

There are a number of third-party companies now offering to manage your ad campaigns. Realize that they will promise the world and end up making it more complicated. Third party software is delayed and optimized on their end to spend less time on you. Honestly, they don't care about your business because they are not invested in it. When it comes to outsourcing effectively it's better you hire staff to work under your own direction. Train them and set them to report their work directly to you.

MORE PASSIVE INCOME

There are so many more ways to monetize your books and make even more passive income! We begin with ACX or Audible which is the audiobook version of KDP. Here you can publish your book in audio format. ACX makes it possible to find narrators, have your book published and then start making sales. Once your book has been released on Amazon it's time to head over to ACX and get it on there. Note ACX is currently only available to citizens of the USA, U.K., Canada, and Australia.

Getting your book on ACX is simple. Click the add new title link and then search for your book. Unless you already have a narrator, you can just click that you're searching for one. Sign the exclusivity agreement for seven years. Note this can be changed a year from now if you want to go wide. More on that later. For now, follow the steps and add in the required information.

For the blurb you might need to cut it down

because Audible offers less words for it. But that's fine. Simply take out some bullet points or less important information. In addition, change any words such as "book" or "reading" to "audiobook" and "listening". Continue to select the genre, owner of copyright - which would be your pen name and year - which would be this year. It's up to you which gender you want to make auditions available for. Go with what works best in that niche. Finally, you can enter the audition script. For this I suggest using your blurb.

On the next page you have the option to enter chapter names. Import those from Amazon and make sure it all makes sense. Move on to the next page where you can send the book to be approved for auditions. Within a day or two ACX will notify you that your book is available for auditions. Keep an eye on your inbox and promotions for this email. Once your book is approved it will be made available for narrators to submit their auditions. Allow at least one week for auditions to come in. Additionally you can search the database for narrators.

An important point is to keep an ear out for some narrators who might be using AI software. Avoid them because it doesn't sound natural. Also avoid any low-quality narration. Identify a high-quality narrator. Yes, they will cost more but ultimately it will lead to more sales. Now if you're on a budget then you can enter a royalty split agreement. <u>But only do this if your super</u>

<u>broke.</u> Otherwise, I highly recommend paying your narrator upfront to ensure you keep all the royalties and have a more flexible contract. Once you find a narrator, send them an offer which can be anything starting at fifty dollars per finished hour. If necessary, negotiate with them. Then it's over to them to produce your book within the range you set. Allow one week for the first fifteen minutes and one month for completing a thirty-thousand-word book.

Once they complete the book, have a listen through it. Confirm that the retail audio sample is good. Again for this you can use the blurb read out or a sample from the book. Once you're happy, upload your nicely optimized Audible cover. Confirm the quality is good and then submit it for approval which takes around fourteen business days.

Pricing

Since ACX doesn't allow you to price your book then you can aim for the sweet spot of having a three hour plus book. Let your narrator know you want that length and that you want them to produce high quality work. Generally, one hour is about 10,000 words.

Here is the pricing on Audible.

- Under 1 hour: $3.95 to $7.00
- 1-3 hours: $7 to $10
- 3-5 hours: $10 to $20

- 5-10 hours: $15 to $25
- 10-20 hours: $20 to $30
- Over 20 hours: $25 to $35

Nonexclusive

As I mentioned earlier when you upload and sign an agreement with ACX it is exclusive for seven years. In an exclusive deal you receive forty percent whilst ACX receive sixty percent. Should you switch to a non-exclusive agreement then you will receive twenty five percent to seventy five percent. For the first year you are tied into this agreement. After one year, check your sales. If any of your books has stopped selling, then it makes sense to go non-exclusive and gain more royalties elsewhere. To opt out of this just send an email to ACX and request opting out. Wait for them to give you approval and then you can go wide. Note if you are in any royalty split with a narrator then this is probably not possible.

Launching an audiobook

Launching an audiobook is quite simple. Since Audible is mostly passive there is little you can do to influence sales. The key point here is to make sure you produce the best quality book you can. Great cover, amazing narrator and optimized blurb. Ultimately the biggest factor is to make sure you are in a niche that is high in demand and low in competition.

To launch the book, make use of the free promo

codes ACX gives you. These allow listeners to download a free copy of the book and this incentives them to leave a review. Send these out to your subscribers. Adjust the email chain you used earlier on to fit this purpose. Additionally share codes in Facebook groups and across social media channels. There are also many code sharing groups. It's also a great idea to create a video of the book. Use the retail audio sample along with some images or clips to promote the release. Good luck!

Even more money

Outside of KDP and ACX there is a whole world of other platforms to publish on which can help to maximize your books potential. We call this going wide. Sometimes your book might not sell on the traditional platforms, but maybe it will elsewhere. Plus, there are some more lucrative ways to milk the money from your books on KDP and ACX. Here I will list some of the platforms and actions you can use to make even more money from your books.

IngramSpark

IngramSpark is a huge platform that distributes books to libraries, bookstores, and various smaller platforms. Not only that but they publish books in regions including the USA, U.K, Australia and many more. For sure you can really make a decent income from Ingram Spark and it's easy to do that. Once your book has gone live you can publish it in paperback and hardcover formats on Ingram Spark. For now I would suggest just a paperback. Use the same data as you input into Amazon. The only additional things you will need are an ISBN and some extra keywords. For the ISBN you can buy a bunch of ISBNs from various websites. Just make sure they are legit and for your region. Yes they can be expensive but it's worth it. For the extra keywords you can use some from your ad campaigns that are relevant. Ingram allows more keywords, and you can enter those together with a semicolon between each keyword.

For the formats and covers you will need to embed fonts which is easy to do within Microsoft Word. Follow these settings. For pricing go with $19.99 and up. Set pricing to $24.99 in Canada and Australia. Select 55% split and destroy if sent back. For release date select one day from now. On the last page you will be requested to pay $49.99 for a submission. I suggest you sign up for a yearly package to ibpaa. For about one hundred and forty dollars per year, they will give you five free promo codes per month along with many other benefits.

Google Play & Draft 2 Digital

These two websites are where you can upload eBook versions of your books for more sales. Both can make a steady and consistent income. Before uploading any of your books here make sure they are not currently enrolled in KDP select. Enrollment into

KDP Select lasts ninety days and you will have to opt out of it. Make sure that period is over and then you can then upload to Google Play and Draft 2 Digital using the same data and files.

Findaway Voices & Authors Republic

These two websites are where you can upload audiobook versions of your books for even more passive income. First make sure they are currently listed as non-exclusive on ACX. Wait one year until the sales release on Audible then request opting out of it via email. Furthermore, only do this with books that have stopped selling on Audible. If it meets these criteria, then you may as well publish them on these platforms. Use the same files. In some cases, they might ask you for proof of rights. Just send them a screenshot or video of the books inside of your ACX account.

Translations

Translating your book is a great way to increase its sales. I've had books that sold nothing on Amazon. So I translated them, and they sold much more. The best language to translate to is Spanish which is one of the most popular languages on Amazon. To translate your books, find a good service on Fiverr, Upwork or even use some of the writing companies. Once it has been delivered, hire a native speaker to read and edit it if necessary. Next you will want to translate your metadata, cover, title, and keywords. Then you're good to launch the book with ads in regions wherever the language is spoken. For audiobooks, have a new native speaker record the book.

Bundles

An amazing feature for self-publishers is to bundle their books. This offers a great value proposition to customers as well as the option to create more revenue for you. It's possible to bundle two books or more together. But note that you can only do this with a book once. To bundle books, create a new title, description, and cover. Highlight that it is a bundle in the cover, title and blurb. Note that Amazon might take objection to the word "bundle" on the paperback or hardcover version. If they do, just remove or replace the word "bundle" with "collection" or something like that. When you create a bundle on ACX you can simply upload your old audio files. The only extra part is to create a new opening and closing chapter with the new title information. Hire the original narrator or another one for that purpose.

STANDING ON THE SHOULDERS OF GIANTS

Just a few years ago, you could easily publish a book under any name and make decent money from it. These days building a brand is essential to succeeding with self-publishing. Now that's a good thing because it's going to ensure that you mine more revenue from your books. Keep in mind how much potential your keywords have for you to spin off into similar topics and leverage more revenue. For example, you could do a "for kids" version or a "for mother's" version and so on. In addition, you can then get into bundles and series where you offer your books as a special edition or as a few books in one. Always keep in mind the potential for more books from any keyword. Ultimately it is more revenue and authority for you. Truly this is the way to stand on the shoulders of giants. So those are the advantages of building a brand, but what goes into building a brand?

Identity

Great brands have a strong identity. They are consistent and recognizable in their presentation. Perception forms a strong connection with customers. When applying these principles to self-publishing the first thing you would need to consider is having a personality or face associated with your brand. Now you don't necessarily have to use your own face. With the help of artificial intelligence you can create a unique face. Visit www.thisisnotarealperson.com to create faces of made-up people. However you will only get one image of this made up person so there is a limit there. If you're serious about building a brand, then you might want to consider using your own face. For fiction brands having a face is essential. For nonfiction brands you can always create a company identity. Although many benefit from having a real personality for customers to relate to.

Design

With a face behind the brand, you want to then work on creating a strong design theme. The number one way to do this is through having a consistent style of book covers. Whether that is using certain colors or style formats. Make it all clearly brandable. For example, look at the way the "Rich Dad, Poor Dad" series uses the same colors and designs. It's instantly recognizable and causes you to associate with the positive message of the brand. Furthermore, there is also a specific style of communication within those books. This can be achieved by working with the same team of writers. Find your winning team and grow it.

Supporting materials

The last cool thing about building a brand is that it can expand outside of Amazon. More revenue and power are in your hands here. So, what does that mean? First of all it's about building a customer list. Then it's about expanding into email marketing, websites, social media, and places where people can find out more about your brand. Creating more content and engaging with your customers helps to forge a stronger brand identity. Whether that's creating videos, infographics or images and so on for your customers. Again, it's all going into the brand and funnels back into making more sales and authority which inevitably leads to more success. Personally, through doing this I have had TV shows contact my brands, customers send loving emails, great sales and much more.

Focus on building an amazing brand. Naturally you won't have enough time and resources to go in on more than a handful of brands. That would stretch yourself too thin. Milk your main brand for everything you can. Research what your competitors are doing and try to do it better. Find the best ways to keep engaging with your customers.

Here are some things to consider.

Email list

Every good brand has an email list. Use it to market your products such as sending your latest book releases and so on. Emails can be collected from having a lead magnet in your books. A lead magnet is essentially a one-page offer you put into your book which should entice your readers to give up their email address in exchange for something of value. So, what can you offer them in your lead magnet? Well there are several things you could offer. Maybe it's a free template, a video, a cheat sheet or a free eBook. Come up with something you feel would be valuable to your readers and that you are happy to offer for free. Keep it as simple as possible. Usually, you would have an intriguing header or statement and then a cool image with a click to find out more. Keep testing these and aim for success rates of at least twenty percent.

Websites such as Mailer Lite make it easy to build a landing page that is linked from the book's lead magnet. Furthermore, keeping it all inside MailerLite enables you to build groups of customer emails which you can send automated emails to. Once you have their email you can set up an automation system to send them their freebie which was offered. You can then also set up a future chain of emails to market to them. Personally, I send daily emails which contain excerpts of my books along with links to buy them. I also regularly send out offers such as when my books are on promotion or when I have new releases. Email marketing software makes that easy to do. Again, I recommend MailerLite which costs just twenty dollars per month. For that you have almost unlimited subscribers, emails, and the ability to create multiple landing pages.

YouTube

YouTube can be a great extension to your brand. Some brands will work well with creating videos. For my main brand I have a team who create and upload videos every week. The goal is to make the YouTube channel monetized, build a strong brand identity and market our books. This is a great addition and by running YouTube ads we can attract even more customers to our books.

Courses & more

Many people enjoy going more in depth with the content of books. Courses present a very cool and interactive way of achieving that. Some brands work well to offer a course as an extra learning resource and revenue for you. In a few days using either yourself or some slides with text you could easily film the content of a course based on your book. Make sure it is of great value and not just a rehash of a book. In addition you could even use your books simply as a lead magnet to selling your course. Many people do that and utilize email marketing to first gather emails from books and then upsell to courses. There is a funnel system and your value proposition. For example, the book is free which leads to the course which is twenty dollars which leads to the advanced course of two hundred dollars which leads to coaching of five hundred dollars which leads to mentorship of five thousand dollars which leads to events and so on.

Social media and websites

Social media channels and websites are always great additions to any brand. Make use of them. Build a website to contain all your books and information about them. Websites are easy, quick and cheap to make nowadays. Just buy a domain name, hosting and make a simple WordPress site or hire someone to do it. Keep updating the blog section to help you rank on Google. Keep your social media updated. Create a Facebook group for your customers to interact with and to share interesting news with.

BUSINESS SETUP & TAX OPTIMIZATION STRATEGIES

Now depending on where you are from this advice is going to vary. For most of us we want to optimize our tax situation. Setting up a company is a great way to do that because it allows you to deduct several expenses such as a manager's salary, company expenses and much more. Each year you will need to file a report of your income and expenses. In the United States there are states such as Wyoming which offer very effective tax setups even for non-residents. Tax is an advanced topic which varies depending on the individual and their own unique circumstances. Ultimately it's always best to seek professional advice from accountants and lawyers.

As I mentioned earlier there are only four countries which ACX currently allows. Those are Canada, USA, U.K and Australia. Now you can set up a company in one of those countries and potentially get access to ACX. But it's not guaranteed. In the past many self-publishers have done this for many years. However recently ACX have been randomly asking for a passport from those countries. So just be aware of that and consult with them if that's your plan. Amazon on the other hand is open to all residents. ACX maybe will be more open later. The industry is always changing and new platforms are on the rise such as Findaway voices recently partnering with Spotify to create audiobooks. Remember to never rely too much on any one of those platforms. Always keep upto date, stay flexible to changes, work hard and stay smart.

Banking

There are many good options for banks these days. If you're in your home country, then a business bank account would be a great start. Make sure they offer a credit card and decent exchange rates. Shop around. If you want to go with online banking then a few I recommend are Wise, Mercury and Payoneer. A note of caution, always make sure you have back up bank accounts, crypto or savings accounts to spread your money just in case there is ever a problem. Don't put all your eggs in one basket.

Virtual assistants

As your business becomes more profitable it's a good idea to start outsourcing some of the smaller tasks so that you can develop new bigger ideas and revenue streams. Self-publishing can become a very passive business allowing you freedom to expand into other business, scale operations, write more books or live more life. Virtual assistants are your answers to making the business more passive. For as little as five dollars per hour you can hire a VA to handle anything from accounting, to ads, keywords research and much more. Hiring one is simple and I highly recommend hiring someone from the Philippines. They are hardworking, speak great English and work for an affordable price.

Head over to [Online Jobs PH](#) and register an account for just seventy dollars. Post a job that specifies what you want them to do. For my VA she does keyword research, formatting, and various other admin tasks. Post the job specifying all of the tasks and create a simple test. This could be something such as a short research test. Once you have narrowed down your candidates, set up a Skype interview with them. Choose the one you feel has the most potential and whom you vibe with. Young up and coming talent is always good to hire because you can shape and mold them to your ways.

Work methods

To train your VA make use of Loom where you can record explainer videos for them to watch. This is time efficient training. For task management I recommend Notion. Each day I use it to enter in and prioritize tasks. Top priority is their focus. In addition, I have them create a daily work diary where they enter their hours and what they worked on each day. This gives me direct feedback and doesn't require constant chatting with them. At any point if I do need to contact them then I can do so directly on either Skype or Slack. Currently I have five virtual assistants. My main one manages them, and we continue to expand and add value.

[VA Template training and contact me for the VA hiring process on my website](https://fortuneselfpublishing.com/coaching/)
https://fortuneselfpublishing.com/coaching/

CONCLUSION

Thanks for reading this book! I hope you've gained some value or at least been inspired to take action. Whether that's self-publishing your first book you've written or taking steps towards being an entrepreneur. At this point I would like to summarize the most important topics covered and give you some key takeaways.

We began this book with keyword research. This is a crucial step of the self-publishing process. Get it right and you will see amazing success. Rush it or don't do it properly and you will see lackluster results. Take your time here and carefully follow the steps. Yes, it can be quite a technical and tedious step but it's the most important step. Do your best to enjoy it and apply your best effort. After keyword research, move onto the steps that I have discussed in this book. Outsourcing this process is fine too. However, if you're a beginner it's always a good idea to invest the time into learning every step of the way. Ultimately it will help you to understand your book more. Follow the nine steps in this book again and again. Revisit them to gain more knowledge.

Publishing a book doesn't require a huge amount of money or a deal with a publisher. As you have seen it is possible for anyone to publish a book. Whether you are an entrepreneur or author my advice will help you to succeed. However, there is a caveat to all of this, and I really want to drive that point home to you here.

Quality is what will make you stand out.

There are other methods which focus on producing quantity and making money. However, that is not the system that I'm offering here. Produce high quality books only and that begins with writing amazing content. Whether that's hiring the best writer you can or maximizing your own talent for writing. Along with writing the best quality book you need to make sure it is delivered with an outstanding cover, formatting, title and descriptions. When you nail all those elements one hundred percent then success is pretty much guaranteed.

Ultimately this is a journey along which the results will be measured by money, success, and feedback from your customers. In the beginning unless you're lucky you're not likely to have outrageous success. Give yourself at least a year to try this all out. Work on learning all of the steps and mastering them. We are living in an age that is thirsty for new content and the best content rises to the top. Work on being in the top ten percent who are making the big bucks and having the most success. Success compounds and if you stick with it then you will see success. Now is the time to get started on your self-publishing journey. Start that book today and if you want my help then get in touch.

<https://fortuneselfpublishing.com/>

ABOUT ME

I began my self-publishing journey in 2017. For the previous five years I had been living overseas working in various jobs to make ends meet. But I was always stuck. I had ambitions to travel more, make more money and to have more freedom. How could I achieve all this? There were people in my social circle who had achieved such things. Some traded, some did affiliate marketing. But all of it seemed so mystical to me. Nevertheless, I jumped in and started testing things out with the little money I had.

I tried Forex trading and broke even after a year. I bought Bitcoin at the peak of 2017 and lost it six months later when the exchange folded. I tried building websites and selling digital products. I tried selling courses. I tried self-publishing and then forgot about it. About a year after self-publishing my first two books which were like forty pages each I came back and checked how much they had made. They hadn't made much but they had made something! Knowing this unlocked my mind to the possibilities. I realized that if I could make just one dollar online then I could make a hundred, two hundred, a thousand and so on. So, I went all in. I worked at night to make ends meet and spent long days trying out self-publishing. Frankly my results were all over the place. I made some horrible books but slowly my income grew. I networked with other self-publishers, hired coaches, studied courses and went all in.

In 2019 I was offered a job which paid well and had little hours. Before my income was all over the place. Now was my chance to steadily invest into my self-publishing business. The contract was for one year and so I set myself the goal to be living from my self-publishing income within one year. That year was a grind of long days. I wrote my own books, hired ghostwriters to write more books, studied courses, learned with coaches and spent my days all in on self-publishing. At night I worked a job using any money I made investing into self-publishing. I didn't care if it was going to make money right away. I was ready to take the risk and go all in. It paid off. In February 2020 right when Covid hit my income was more than my job. The job offered me half salary and more hours because of Covid. But I had my ticket out. That's the beauty of it, freedom to do what you want. I resigned and since then my income has tripled. I have been able to live in South America, Asia, Europe and anywhere I want. Time zone is not important to me. I make smart decisions and continue to reap the rewards. That is true passive income and that is **freedom**.

https://fortuneselfpublishing.com/

BONUS CONTENT

I currently offer limited spots for one-on-one coaching. But it is only for those serious about scaling their business to the next level. If that sounds like you then follow or click the link below.

https://fortuneselfpublishing.com/coaching/

I also offer several resources for helping on my website including freebies, templates, advice and much more. Follow or click the link below.

https://fortuneselfpublishing.com/

https://www.subscribepage.com/fortunepublishing

Or scan the QR code below.

RESOURCES

1. Bookbeam
   https://bookbeam.io/?ref=69
2. Canva
   https://partner.canva.com/JrMqkv
3. Fiverr
   https://track.fiverr.com/visit/?bta=545061&nci=9496
4. Fortune Self-Publishing
   https://fortuneselfpublishing.com/
5. Hot Ghost Writer
   https://hotghostwriter.com/
6. KDP Rocket
   https://publisherrocket.com/
7. KDSPY
   https://jvz4.com/c/2679265/111047/
8. Mailerlite
   https://www.mailerlite.com/
9. Microsoft Word
   https://www.microsoft.com
10. Online Jobs PH
    http://store.onlinejobs.ph/?aid=416661
11. Pubby
    https://pubby.co/?invite=17187
12. The Urban Writers
    https://theurbanwriters.com/
13. The Writing Summit
    https://thewritingsummit.com/

OTHER BOOKS BY WILLIAM SWAIN

Available now in Ebook, Paperback, Hardcover, and Audiobook in all regions.

FORTUNE SELF-PUBLISHING

We sincerely hope you enjoyed our new book **"Fortune Self-Publishing"**. We would greatly appreciate your feedback with an honest review at the place of purchase.

First and foremost, we are always looking to grow and improve as a team. It is reassuring to hear what works, as well as receive constructive feedback on what should improve. Second, starting out as an unknown author is exceedingly difficult, and Amazon reviews go a long way toward making the journey out of anonymity possible. Please take a few minutes to write an honest review.

Best regards,
William Swain

www.ingramcontent.com/pod-product-compliance
Lightning Source LLC
Chambersburg PA
CBHW050030130526
44590CB00042B/2434